W9-BBP-876

DATE DUE

Gone Forever!
Pterodactyl

Rupert Matthews

Heinemann Library
Chicago, Illinois

Designed by Ron Kamen and Paul Davies & Associates
Illustrations: by James Field (SGA) and Darren Lingard
Originated by Ambassador Litho Ltd
Printed and bound in China by South China Printing Company

07 06 05 04 03
10 9 8 7 6 5 4 3 2 1
Library of Congress Cataloging-in-Publication Data

Matthews, Rupert.
    Pterodactyl / Rupert Matthews.
        p. cm. -- (Gone forever)
Summary: Describes what has been learned about the physical features,
behavior, and surroundings of the long-extinct pterodactyl.
Includes bibliographical references and index.
    ISBN 1-40340-790-8 (HC), 1-4034-3418-2 (Pbk)
    1. Pterodactyls--Juvenile literature. [1. Pterodactyls. 2.
Dinosaurs.] I. Title. II. Gone forever (Heinemann Library)
    QE862.P7 M37 2003
    567.918--dc21
                                    2002003700
Acknowledgments
The author and publishers are grateful to the following for permission to reproduce copyright material:
pp. 4, 16, 18, 26 Peter Morris/Ardea; p.6 Corbis; pp. 8, 12, 20 Natural History Museum, London; p.10 Claude Nuridsany and Marie Perennou/Science Photo Library; pp. 14, 22 D. M. Unwin/Museum für Naturkunde, Berlin; p. 24 Visuals Unlimited.
Cover photo reproduced with permission of The Natural History Museum, London.

Special thanks to Dr. Peter Mackovicky for his review of this book.

Every effort has been made to contact copyright holders of any material reproduced in this book. Any omissions will be rectified in subsequent printings if notice is given to the publishers.

Some words are shown in bold, **like this.** You can find out what they mean by looking in the glossary.

Contents

Gone Forever!

Many different types of animals lived millions of years ago. Most of them are now **extinct.** This means that they have all died. The **fossils** of some of these animals have been found in rocks.

pterodactyl fossil

4

One of the extinct animals was pterodactyl. Its fossil bones show that this was a **reptile** that could fly. There were other types of flying reptiles, called **pterosaurs,** that lived at the same time.

Pterodactyl's Home

Scientists have found the **fossil** bones of pterodactyls in rocks in Germany, a country in Europe. The rocks also have plant fossils. The rocks tell us what the land was like when the pterodactyl was alive.

8

Pterodactyls lived in places along the edges of warm seas that were not very deep. There were many sandy beaches. The land was covered with thick forests. The weather was hot and dry.

Life at Sea

Many types of animals lived in the seas when pterodactyls were living. We know about these animals because scientists have found their **fossils.** The fossils are in the rocks formed at the bottom of the sea.

fossil of an Ichthyosaurus

8

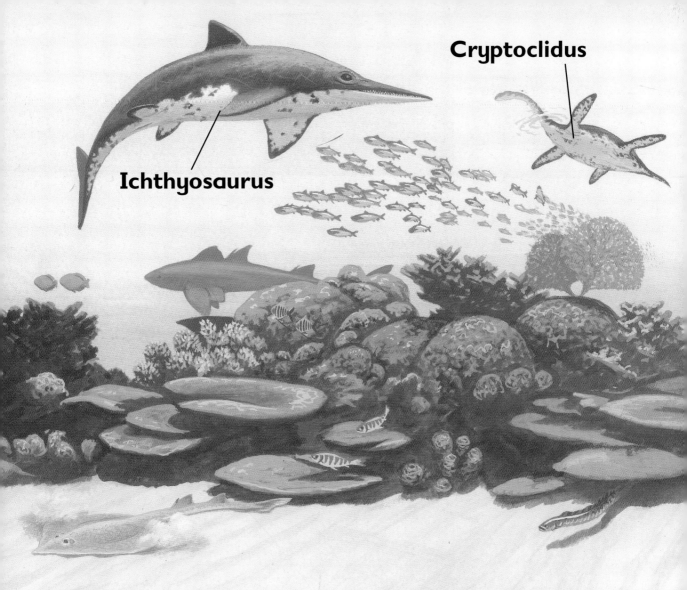

Cryptoclidus

Ichthyosaurus

There were many different types of fish. Some of them looked like fish today. There were also giant **reptiles.** **Ichthyosaurus** was a reptile that looked and swam like a fish. **Cryptoclidus** had a long neck. It swam using strong legs shaped like paddles.

Life on Land

Pterodactyls lived at the same time as the **dinosaurs.** The **fossils** of other animals show us that there were many types of insects living around that time, too.

dragonfly fossil

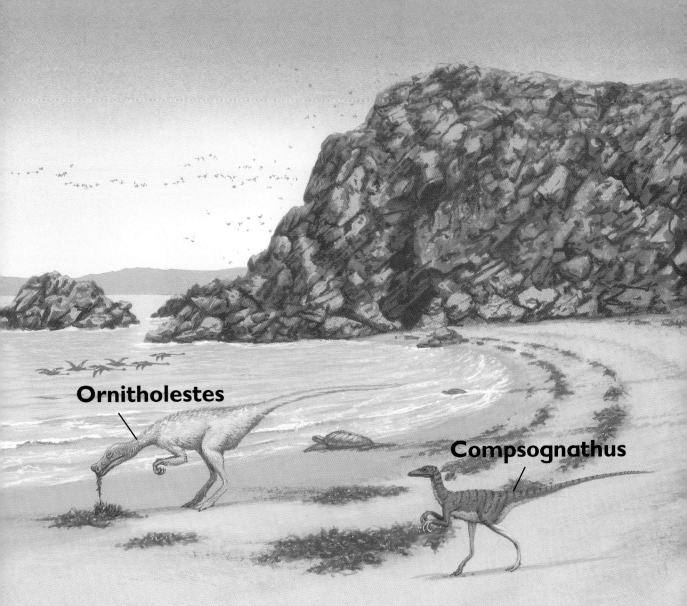

Ornitholestes

Compsognathus

There were many different types of land animals.
There were small hunting dinosaurs, such as
Ornitholestes and **Compsognathus**. They ate
lizards and other small animals.

11

What Was Pterodactyl?

Pterodactyls were small, flying **reptiles.** Their wings were made of skin that was like leather. The wings were about 16 inches long, from tip to tip. A pterodactyl's body was likely covered with fur to help keep it warm.

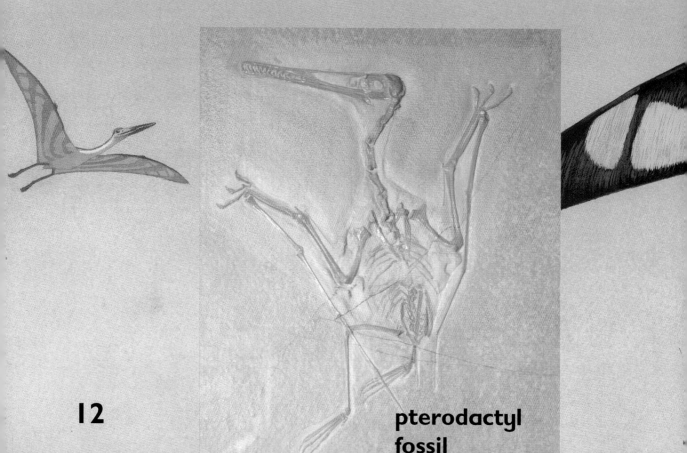

pterodactyl fossil

Scientists have found many pterodactyl **fossils.** In some cases, they have found the skin as well as the bones. These tell us what pterodactyl was like and how it lived.

A Cliff-Top Home

fossil of a baby pterodactyl

Pterodactyls may have laid their eggs on cliffs. There, they would have been safe from **dinosaurs,** such as **Ornitholestes.** Perhaps the eggs were laid on nests made of leaves and moss. Maybe one pterodactyl parent sat on the nest while the other searched for food.

14

Pterodactyl babies were probably cared for by their parents. The adults probably brought food to the babies. After a few weeks the young would have been old enough to fly. Young pterodactyls might have hunted insects.

On the Wing

The **fossil** wings of a pterodactyl tell us how it could fly. The bones were hollow. This made them light but strong. Strong muscles could move the wings quickly.

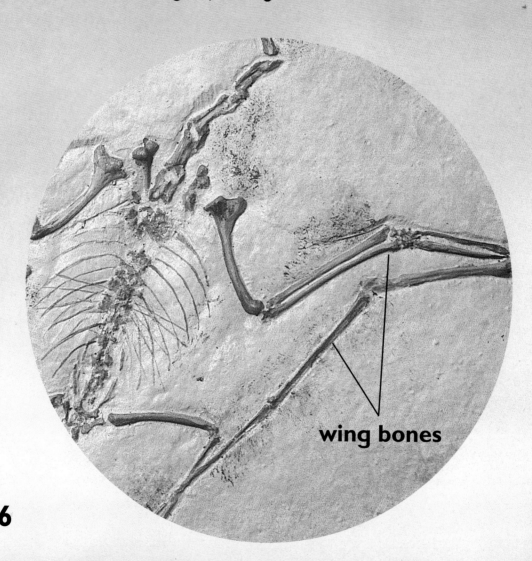

wing bones

Pterodactyls were good at flying. They could change direction easily. They could dive or climb quickly. Pterodactyls could probably fly for quite a long time before they had to land and rest.

Crawling

The legs of a pterodactyl were thin and weak. They probably did not have strong muscles. Pterodactyls would have been slow when moving on the ground.

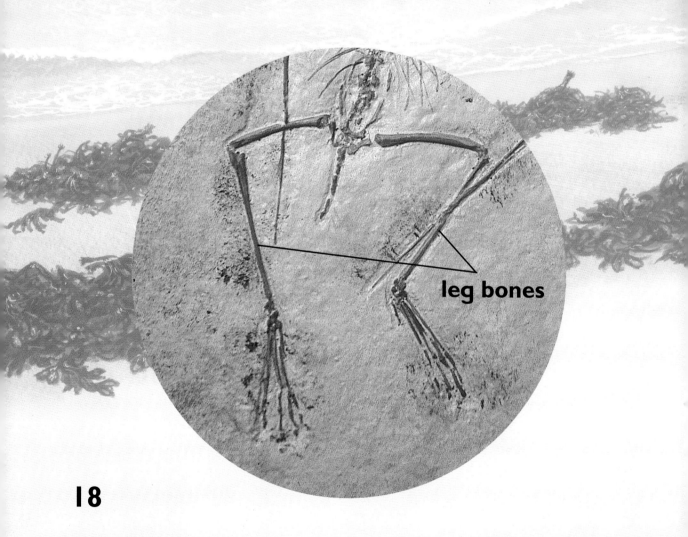

leg bones

Some scientists think a pterodactyl walked on its wings and legs. It would have folded its wings and rested on the claws on its front.legs. Other scientists think a pterodactyl could have walked just on its back legs. But this is not likely.

19

Finding Food

eye

Fossil skulls of pterodactyls
show us they had very large eyes.
This means they probably could see
well. Pterodactyls used this good
sight to find food as they flew.

20

Sometimes, pterodactyls looked for food on beaches. They hunted for worms in the mud. At other times, pterodactyls flew through the air. They snapped up insects as they flew.

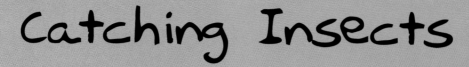

Catching Insects

Pterodactyls had long **jaws** filled with sharp, pointed teeth. The teeth pointed forward. These teeth would have been good for catching large insects.

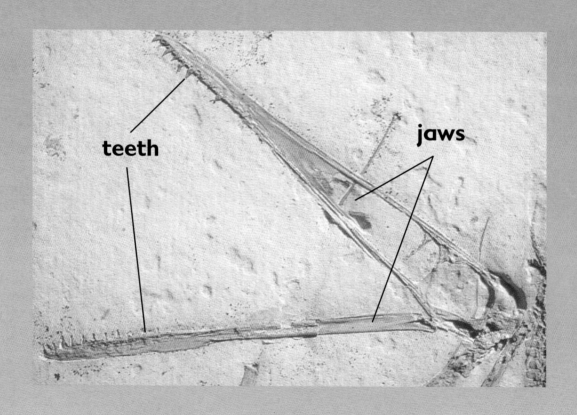

teeth

jaws

A pterodactyl caught insects in the air. It snapped its jaws shut so that its teeth closed on the **prey.** A pterodactyl may have eaten small insects in one piece.

Danger!

Other animals probably hunted pterodactyls.
One of these animals may have been
Cryptoclidus. Cryptoclidus was a **reptile.**

fossil of a Cryptoclidus

Cryptoclidus lived in the sea. It could raise its head above the water. If a pterodactyl did not see the sea reptile in time, it might be eaten!

Other Flying Creatures

There were other flying animals at around the same time as pterodactyls. One of these was **Archaeopteryx.** Archaeopteryx had feathers. It is one of the earliest birds.

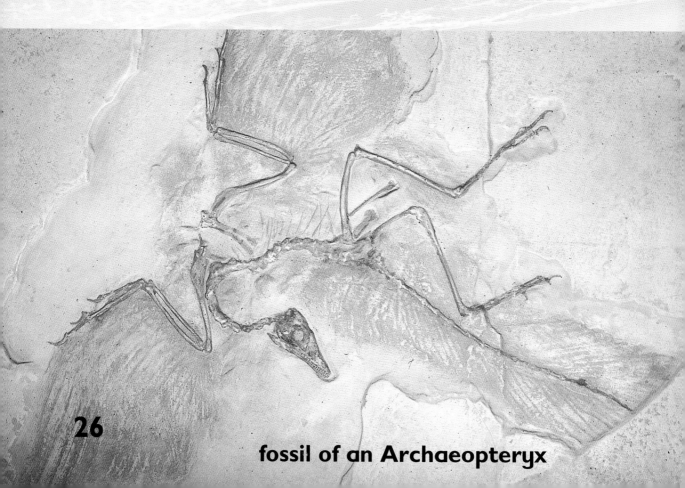

fossil of an Archaeopteryx

Birds like Archaeopteryx hunted insects. Millions of years later, birds became more common than flying **reptiles.** The flying reptiles became **extinct.** Many different kinds of birds are still alive today.

27

Where Did Pterodactyls Live?

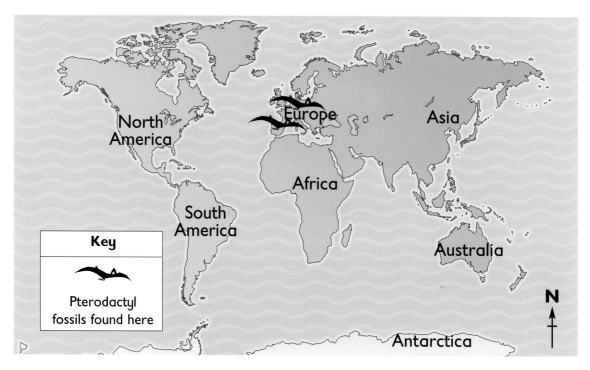

Pterodactyls lived in what is now Europe.
At the time, much of western Europe lay below
a wide sea. But there was some dry land.
Pterodactyls lived along the coast of Europe.

When Did Pterodactyls Live?

Pterodactyls lived between 160 and 142 million years ago. They lived during the Age of **Dinosaurs.** All flying **reptiles** became **extinct** at the same time that dinosaurs became extinct.

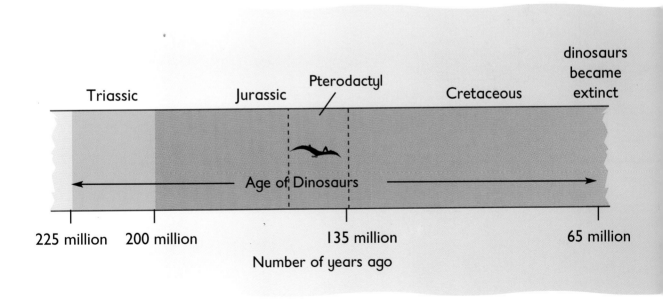

Triassic   Jurassic   Pterodactyl   Cretaceous   dinosaurs became extinct

Age of Dinosaurs

225 million   200 million   135 million   65 million

Number of years ago

Fact File

Pterodactyl	
Wingspan:	16 inches (40 centimeters)
Weight:	4-7 ounces (100–200 grams)
Time:	About 150 million years ago
Place:	Europe

How to Say It

Archaeopteryx—ar-key-op-ter-rix
Compsognathus—komp-sog-nay-thus
Cryptoclidus—kripp-toe-klee-duss
dinosaur—dine-ah-sor
Ichthyosaurus—ick-thee-ah-sor-us
Ornitholestes—or-ni-tho-less-teez
pterodactyl—ter-ra-dak-till

Glossary

Archaeopteryx one of the first known birds. Archaeopteryx lived about 150 million years ago.

Compsognathus small dinosaur that ran on two legs. It hunted small animals for food.

Cryptoclidus large reptile that lived in the sea and swam using its four flippers

dinosaur one of a large group of reptiles that lived on Earth millions of years ago.

extinct no longer living on Earth

fossil remains of a plant or animal, usually found inside rocks. Most fossils are hard parts like bones or teeth. Some fossils are traces of animals, such as their footprints.

Ichthyosaurus reptile that lived in the sea

jaw part of the mouth which holds the teeth

lizard small reptile that moves on four legs

nostril openings in the nose through which air is breathed in and out

Ornitholestes small hunting dinosaur that had strong front claws

prey animal that is hunted and eaten by another animal

pterosaur type of extinct reptile. It had wings made of skin and could fly. There were many different types of pterosaurs.

reptile cold-blooded animal, usually with scaly skin. Snakes, lizards and turtles are all reptiles. Dinosaurs were reptiles, too.

skull bones of the head

More Books to Read

Zimmerman, Howard. *Dinosaurs: The Biggest, Baddest, Strangest, Fastest.* New York: Atheneum, 2000.
Zimmerman, Howard. *Beyond the Dinosaurs!* New York: Atheneum, 2001.

An older person can help you read this book.
Holmes, Thom and Laurie. *Prehistoric Flying Reptiles: The Pterosaurs.* Berkeley Heights, NJ.: Enslow Publishers, Inc., 2003.

Index